Animal Dreamers
Art Therapy Coloring Book

illustrated by Daniel de Sosa

BACKWARDSBURD.COM

Published by Backwards Burd Comics.
Fourth printing.

SLAWTH

Burdlife

Backwards Burd is a London based
comics collective. They have exhibited at comic
conventions and zine fairs across the UK, including MCM London, Thought
Bubble, and Comica Comiket in the British Library.
The BB team have been touring across the country for three years, and have
developed a cult following.

Together with their diverse art styles, they
create weird and wonderful comix, merch, and
hand-made zines.

FOLLOW DANIEL DE SOSA ONLINE:

Twitter: @BARDICFURY

IG: desosaink

FACEBOOK.COM/DESOSAINK

SHOP ONLINE AT:

BACKWARDSBURD.COM